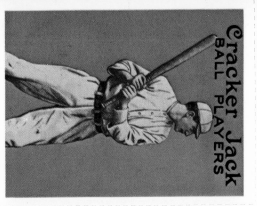

KONETCHY, Pittsburgh - Nationals

Cracker Jack BALL PLAYERS

EVERS, Boston - Nationals

...Jack ...YERS

BRESNAHAN, St. Louis Nat'l

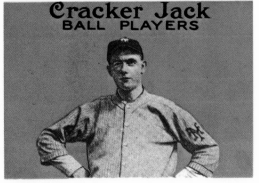

Cracker Jack BALL PLAYERS

MARQUARD, Brooklyn - Federals

DOYLE, New York - Nationals

Cracker Jack BALL PLAYERS

CUBS

M. BROWN, Chicago Nat'l

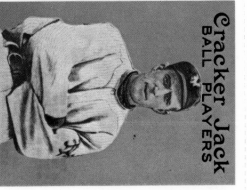

MERKLE, New York - Nationals

Cracker Jack BALL PLAYERS

McGRAW, New York - Nationals

Cracker Jack BALL PLAYERS

N. Y.

MERKLE, N. Y. Nat'l

ADAMS, Pittsburgh - Nationals

Cracker Jack BALL PLAYERS

ZIMMERMAN, Chicago - Nationals

Cracker Jack BALL PLAYERS

John J. Evers
CUBS

Frank L. Chance
CUBS

18

John J. Evers, infielder of the Boston N. L. team, was born in Troy, N. Y., March 21, 1883. He first played baseball with the Troy team in the spring of 1902, beginning in the outfield and being tried at short. He was purchased from the Troy club by the Chicago cubs, September, 1902. Managed Chicago Cubs in 1913. He signed a four-year contract with the Boston Nationals, February 13, 1914.

118

Edward Konetchy, first baseman of the Pittsburgh National League Club, was born in March, 1886, at La Crosse, Wis. In 1905 he began professional play with his home town team in the Wisconsin State League. He was sold to St. Louis Nationals on June 29, 1905. He remained with that team until the fall of 1913, when he was traded to the Pittsburgh Nationals in a big player swap.

4

Lawrence J. Doyle, second baseman of the New York National League team, was born in Caseyville, Ill., July 31, 1886. He was an amateur ball player until 1905, when he joined the Mattoon Club of the "Kitty" League. At the close of the season of 1906 he was bought by the Giants for $4500. He has been the regular second baseman of the team since 1908.

43

Richard W. Marquard, pitcher of the Brooklyn Federal League team, was born in Cleveland, Ohio, April 22, 1889. After the Cleveland Americans had refused him a trial, he obtained a position with the Canton Central League team in 1907. He took part in forty games, and his fine work caused the Indianapolis club to draft him. He played with Indianapolis until 1908, when he was sold to the Giants for $11,000. In fall of 1914 he jumped to Brooklyn Federals.

69

John J. McGraw, manager of the New York National League team, was born in Truxton, N. Y., April 7, 1873. In 1891 he played with the Cedar Rapids Club, then went to the Baltimore Club in 1892, and remained there until 1899. He was sold to the St. Louis Nationals in 1900, and in 1901 he organized a new Baltimore Club and placed it in the American League. In 1902 he sold out the Baltimore Club to the New York Giants. McGraw has been manager of the Giants since 1903.

78

Frederick Merkle, first baseman of the New York National League team, was born in Watertown, Wis., December 20, 1888. He began semi-professional ball as a pitcher in 1906. In that season he was signed by Tecumseh to play third base. He was bought by the New York Club in August, 1907. As a first baseman he has made good in all ways.

21

Henry Zimmerman, infielder of the Chicago National League team, was born in New York City, February 10, 1886. In 1905 he was the star pitcher for the Mindfords of New York. In 1906 he played with the Bronx Athletic and Red Hook teams, and in 1907 went to Wilkes-Barre, Pa. He was bought by the Chicago Cubs August 25, 1907.

63

Charles B. Adams, pitcher of the Pittsburgh National League team, was born in Tipton, Ind., May 18, 1883. In 1905 he signed with a salaried team playing at Parsons, Kan. He next went to the St. Louis Cardinals, and from there to Denver. The Denver team sold him to Pittsburgh in 1907, but he was farmed out to Louisville for the season of 1908. He rejoined Pittsburgh in 1909.

FRANK L. CHANCE

Frank L. Chance joined the Chicago Nationals in 1898. Made manager in 1905, in 1906, 1907, 1908 and 1910, he led them to the National Championship, and in 1907 and 1908 to the world's championship also. Five years he batted over .300. In 1910 on 814 chances he made only three errors, the percentage, .996, being a world's record.

Evers Makes a Safe Slide

The illustration on the other side of the card shows Johnny Evers, Chicago's famous second baseman, making a great slide to third. He is one of the most annoying—to the other side—base stealers among the professionals. He takes long leads, up on his toes all the time, doing a little dance, and edging toward the next base. He is always a good waiter at bat, getting many bases on balls, and generally leads the batting order. Evers was born in Troy, N. Y., in 1883, where he still lives and is president of the John J. Evers Association. He joined the Troy team in 1902 as an outfielder. Then he was drafted to Chicago, where his career is baseball history.

JOHN J. EVERS

Johnnie Evers, the famous second baseman of the Chicago Nationals, is a native of Troy, and went directly to the Cubs from there, in 1902. In 1903 he played second one day, and has ever since been an effective part of the Cubs' machine. He is generally lead-off man in the batting order, being a good waiter. If he fails to get first on a pass, he is likely to arrive on a hit.

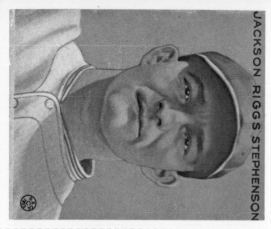

JACKSON RIGGS STEPHENSON

LONNIE WARNEKE

CHARLES (CHUCK) KLEIN

LEWIS (HACK) WILSON

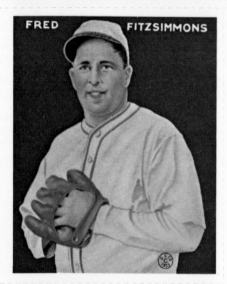

FRED FITZSIMMONS

FRANK (LEFTY) O'DOUL

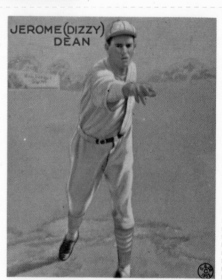

JEROME (DIZZY) DEAN

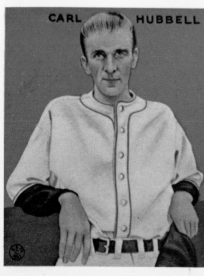

CARL HUBBELL

MELVIN OTT

ADOLFO LUQUE

JESSE HAINES

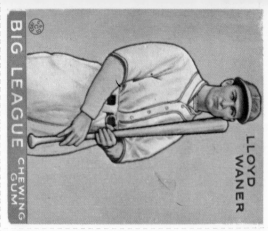

LLOYD WANER

BOB O'FARRELL

ROGERS HORNSBY

JIMMY WILSON

BILL TERRY

"KIKI" CUYLER

"PEPPER" MARTIN

"DUCKY" MEDWICK

JIM BOTTOMLEY

"PEE WEE" REESE

"VINCE" DI MAGGIO

"CHUCK" KLEIN

"JOHNNY" COONEY

HARRY "GUNBOAT" GUMBERT

"BILL" JURGES

60. CHARLES HERBERT KLEIN

Outfielder-Coach   **Philadelphia Phillies**

Born: Indianapolis, Ind.   *October 7, 1905*
Bats: Left   Throws: Right
Height: 6'   Weight: 195 lbs.

One of the most popular players ever to wear a Philadelphia uniform, "Chuck" Klein now splits his duties with the Phillies between coaching, pinch-hitting and an occasional fling in the outfield. His past playing, however, have gained him a set place in baseball annals. The quiet, personable outfielder has been one of the great hitters of modern times, boasting a .324 lifetime average. He has collected 2063 hits, including 299 home runs, and has driven across 1195 runs.

A DOVER REPRINT
PLAY BALL
Sports Hall of Fame

Watch for other famous sports stars, famous fighters, tennis players, football heroes, etc. in this series.
©   GUM, INC., Phila., Pa.   PRINTED IN U.S.A.

---

61. VINCENT PAUL DI MAGGIO

Outfielder   **Pittsburgh Pirates**

Born: Martinez, Cal.   *September 6, 1912*
Bats: Right   Throws: Right
Height: 5' 11½"   Weight: 185 lbs.

Persistence made a good ball player out of "Vince" Di Maggio last year with the Pittsburgh Pirates. Always an asset defensively, with a remarkable throwing arm, "Vince" couldn't seem to hit major league pitching consistently enough to stick, but he batted .289 for the Bucs last year, drove in 54 runs, and hit 19 home runs. He made only 5 errors afield, contributed 13 assists. He was traded in May last year to the Pirates by the Cincinnati Reds.

A DOVER REPRINT
PLAY BALL
Sports Hall of Fame

Watch for other famous sports stars, famous fighters, tennis players, football heroes, etc. in this series.
©   GUM, INC., Phila., Pa.   PRINTED IN U.S.A.

---

54. HAROLD HENRY REESE

Shortstop   **Brooklyn Dodgers**

Born: Ekron, Ky.   *July 23, 1919*
Bats: Right   Throws: Right
Height: 5' 10"   Weight: 162 lbs.

If the signs are right, "Pee Wee" Reese, a young man who cost the Brooklyn Dodgers a reported price of $75,000 in cash and players, is destined to become one of the leading shortstops in the National League. Reese came up to the Dodgers from Louisville last year and proved that he was as brilliant a fielder, as they said he was, and that he could hit on occasion. The real test, however, was halted when he fractured his heel sliding into second base on August 15th, and was out for the rest of the season. There's no doubt any longer about Reese being major league calibre, but how good he really is, remains to be told this year.

A DOVER REPRINT
PLAY BALL
Sports Hall of Fame

Watch for other famous sports stars, famous fighters, tennis players, football heroes, etc. in this series.
©   GUM, INC., Phila., Pa.   PRINTED IN U.S.A.

---

59. WILLIAM FREDERICK JURGES

Shortstop   **New York Giants**

Born: Brooklyn, N. Y.   *May 9, 1908*
Bats: Right   Throws: Right
Height: 5' 11"   Weight: 175 lbs.

A lot of the future of the New York Giants depends on how "Bill" Jurges will go at shortstop this year. Fate can play funny tricks, and it played one on Jurges and the Giants when one of "Bucky" Walters' usually accurate pitches struck Jurges on the head on June 23rd, last year, and put him out for the remainder of the season, depriving the Giants of the most valuable shortstop in the National League. Indications thus far are that Jurges will not only completely recover but will regain the brilliance that made him an outstanding shortstop and a dangerous batter.

A DOVER REPRINT
PLAY BALL
Sports Hall of Fame

Watch for other famous sports stars, famous fighters, tennis players, football heroes, etc. in this series.
©   GUM, INC., Phila., Pa.   PRINTED IN U.S.A.

---

26. HARRY EDWARD GUMBERT

Pitcher   **New York Giants**

Born: Elizabeth, Pa.   *November 5, 1911*
Bats: Right   Throws: Right
Height: 6' 1½"   Weight: 185 lbs.

Harry Gumbert did not set the baseball world on fire with his pitching last year—he was not too good on occasion, but far from bad—but he brought one honor to the New York Giants. Gumbert was the outstanding fielding pitcher in the National League in 1940. In 35 games, Harry did not make an error, while contributing 65 assists. As a pitcher, Harry fell off from his great year in 1939 by winning only 12, against 14 losses. His showing in Spring training has been highly encouraging to "Bill" Terry, however.

A DOVER REPRINT
PLAY BALL
Sports Hall of Fame

Watch for other famous sports stars, famous fighters, tennis players, football heroes, etc. in this series.
©   GUM, INC., Phila., Pa.   PRINTED IN U.S.A.

---

50. JOHN WALTER COONEY

Outfielder   **Boston Braves**

Born: Cranston, R. I.   *March 18, 1901*
Bats: Right   Throws: Left
Height: 5' 10"   Weight: 165 lbs.

One of the greatest of modern defensive outfielders, "Johnny" Cooney is also one of the most durable. Age and years of activity have not seemed to dull either his batting eye or his fielding ability. Last year, he played in 108 games of the Braves, and batted a powerful .318, driving in 21 runs and scoring 40 himself. As an outfielder, he made only 2 errors, with a percentage of .993. Starting as a pitcher, Cooney has been in baseball since 1921. With the exception of three seasons with Brooklyn, he has spent all his major league time with Boston.

A DOVER REPRINT
PLAY BALL
Sports Hall of Fame

Watch for other famous sports stars, famous fighters, tennis players, football heroes, etc. in this series.
©   GUM, INC., Phila., Pa.   PRINTED IN U.S.A.

ENOS SLAUGHTER

Outfield—St. Louis Cardinals
Born: Roxboro, N. C., April 27, 1916
Height: 5-9   Weight: 185
Bats: Left   Throws: Right

"Country" Slaughter, veteran outfielder, had one of best seasons in 1949. His .336 batting average was third best in league. Drove in 96 runs. Hit 34 doubles, 13 triples, 13 homers. Rookie year with Cards: 1938. In service, 1943-1945. In 1946 led National League in runs batted in. Has tremendous fighting spirit. On 6 all-star teams.   A DOVER REPRINT

No. 35 in the 1950 SERIES of BASEBALL Picture Cards
© 1950 Bowman Gum, Inc., Phila., Pa., U.S.A.

ED STANKY

Second Base—New York Giants
Born: Philadelphia, Pa., Sept. 3, 1917
Height: 5-8   Weight: 165
Bats: Right   Throws: Right

Came to Giants from Braves in big winter trade, 1949. Hit stride as player when traded by Cubs to Dodgers during 1944 season. In 1948, traded to pennant-winning Braves. A tip-top lead-off-man. Set up league record for bases on balls with 148 in 1945. Led again in 1946 with 137. In 1947 set up a league fielding record, second basemen (.985).   A DOVER REPRINT

No. 29 in the 1950 SERIES of BASEBALL Picture Cards
© 1950 Bowman Gum, Inc., Phila., Pa., U.S.A.

WARREN SPAHN

Pitcher—Boston Braves
Born: Buffalo, N. Y., April 23, 1922
Height: 6 ft.   Weight: 185
Bats: Left   Throws: Left

Had a great 1949 season with a 21-14 record. Completed most games, 25; pitched most innings, 302; won most games, 21; faced most batters, 1,258; led in strikeouts, 151; tied for starting most games, 38. Before 1949, Warren's biggest year was 1946 when he compiled a 21-10 record. Spent 3 seasons in service. In 1 World's Series. On 2 all-star teams.
No. 19 in the 1950 SERIES of BASEBALL Picture Cards
© 1950 Bowman Gum, Inc., Phila., Pa., U.S.A.
A DOVER REPRINT

RALPH KINER

Outfield—Pittsburgh Pirates
Born: Santa Rita, N. M., Oct. 27, 1922
Height: 6-1½   Weight: 190
Bats: Right   Throws: Right

A great slugger. Last season, with 54 homers, Ralph led the league for the fourth time in his four years in the majors, thus extending a big-time record. Led league in runs batted in, and hit .310. Joined Pirates in 1946. Has hit 168 homers for them, and driven in 458 runs. Started in organized baseball, 1941. 3 years in minors; 3 in service.   A DOVER REPRINT

No. 33 in the 1950 SERIES of BASEBALL Picture Card © 1950 Bowman Gum, Inc., Phila., Pa., U.S.A.

DON NEWCOMBE

Pitcher—Brooklyn Dodgers
Born: Madison, N. J., June 14, 1924
Height: 6-4   Weight: 220
Bats: Left   Throws: Right

One of the outstanding pitchers in the league. Joined Dodgers after 1949 season started, but still had 19–5 record. Appeared in 38 games, pitched 244 innings. Gave up only 223 hits and 73 bases on balls, while striking out 149. Earned-run average (3.17) was third lowest in league. Don pitched 5 shutouts, tying for league lead.   A DOVER REPRINT

No. 23 in the 1950 SERIES of BASEBALL Picture Cards
© 1950 Bowman Gum, Inc., Phila., Pa., U.S.A.

BILL NICHOLSON

Outfield—Philadelphia Phillies
Born: Chestertown, Md., Dec. 11, 1914
Height: 6 ft.   Weight: 200
Bats: Right   Throws: Right

Out of the lineup, because of illness, in the final stages of the 1950 pennant race. But back in tip-top shape for 1951. Started in organized baseball in the Texas League. Came up to the Athletics, then back to minors. Acquired, 1939, by the Chicago Cubs. Tied a major-league record in 1944 by hitting 4 home runs in 4 successive times at bat. Led NL in home runs, 1943 and 1944. Traded to Phils for 1949.

No. 113 in the 1951 SERIES

BASEBALL
PICTURE CARDS

©1951 Bowman Gum, Inc., Phila., Pa., U.S.A.
A DOVER REPRINT

LARRY JANSEN

Pitcher—New York Giants
Born: Verboort, Ore., July 16, 1920
Height: 6-2   Weight: 190
Bats: Right   Throws: Right

Won 19 games in 1950. Lost 13. Tied for League lead in shutouts with 5. Earned run average, 3.01, was fourth lowest for NL. Did a beautiful stint on the mound in the All-Star game. Career began with Salt Lake City in 1940. Came to the Giants in 1947. In rookie year won 21, lost 5, for an .808 percentage. Record in 1948 was 18-12; in 1949 it was 15-16. Control is one of Larry Jansen's strong points.

No. 162 in the 1951 SERIES

BASEBALL
PICTURE CARDS

©1951 Bowman Gum, Inc., Phila., Pa., U.S.A.
A DOVER REPRINT

WES WESTRUM

Catcher—New York Giants
Born: Clearbrook, Minn., Nov. 28, 1922
Height: 5-11   Weight: 190
Bats: Right   Throws: Right

Caught 139 games in 1950—many of them with a badly bruised hand and a charley horse. Reinstated last season, and again slated for relief duty. Made a starter after season was under way. Wound up with 18-4 record for an .818 percentage, best in League, and an earned run average of 2.71—the League's second best. Had an 11-game winning streak. Pitched 4 successive shutouts. Had 5 in all.

No. 161 in the 1951 SERIES

BASEBALL
PICTURE CARDS

©1951 Bowman Gum, Inc., Phila., Pa., U.S.A.
A DOVER REPRINT

SAL MAGLIE

Pitcher—New York Giants
Born: Niagara Falls, N.Y., Apr. 26, 1917
Height: 6-2   Weight: 180
Bats: Right   Throws: Right

A relief pitcher for the Giants before going to Mexican League. Reinstated last season, and again slated for relief duty. Made a starter after season was under way. Wound up with 18-4 record for an .818 percentage, best in League, and an earned run average of 2.71—the League's second best. Had an 11-game winning streak. Pitched 4 successive shutouts. Had 5 in all.

No. 127 in the 1951 SERIES

BASEBALL
PICTURE CARDS

©1951 Bowman Gum, Inc., Phila., Pa., U.S.A.
A DOVER REPRINT

CLYDE McCULLOUGH

Catcher—Pittsburgh Pirates
Born: Nashville, Tenn., March 4, 1918
Height: 5-11½   Weight: 185
Bats: Right   Throws: Right

In 103 games for the Pirates in 1950. Hit .254. Batted in 34 runs. Clyde's first pro experience was in 1935 with Lafayette of the Evangeline League. Came into the majors with the Cubs in 1940. Finished the season with Buffalo. Returned to the Cubs in 1941. Remained with them until traded to the Pirates. Highest batting average was .287 compiled in 1942. In the service 2 years.

No. 94 in the 1951 SERIES

BASEBALL
PICTURE CARDS

©1951 Bowman Gum, Inc., Phila., Pa., U.S.A.
A DOVER REPRINT

EMIL "DUTCH" LEONARD

Pitcher—Chicago Cubs
Born: Auburn, Ill., March 25, 1910
Height: 6-1   Weight: 200
Bats: Right   Throws: Right

The 1950 season was the 20th in organized baseball for popular "Dutch" Leonard. He began in 1930, and made the majors, at the end of the 1933 campaign, with the Brooklyn Dodgers. Remained with them until 1936. Then sent to minors for 2 seasons. With Washington Senators, 1938-1946. Spent 1947 and 1948 with the Phillies. With Cubs since 1949. Had 5-1 record, 1950.   A DOVER REPRINT

No. 102 in the 1951 SERIES

BASEBALL
PICTURE CARDS

©1951 Bowman Gum, Inc., Phila., Pa., U.S.A.

PHIL CAVARRETTA

First Base, Outfield—Chicago Cubs
Born: Chicago, Ill., July 19, 1917
Height: 5-11   Weight: 183
Bats: Left   Throws: Left

Phil—the Cubs' captain—has been with the team 16 full seasons. Kept out of action by an injury during much of 1950. In only 82 games. But he batted .273, and his hits included 11 doubles and 10 home runs. He drove in 31 tallies. Phil's best season was 1945 when he paced the National League with a .355 batting average, and got the most valuable player nod. Popular at home and on road.

No. 138 in the 1951 SERIES

BASEBALL
PICTURE CARDS

©1951 Bowman Gum, Inc., Phila., Pa., U.S.A.
A DOVER REPRINT

HAROLD "PEEWEE" REESE

Shortstop—Brooklyn Dodgers
Born: Ekron, Ky., July 23, 1919
Height: 5-10   Weight: 168
Bats: Right   Throws: Right

"Peewee" Reese is a great fielding shortstop. Holds many records that prove his ability. Had an off-season in 1950, as far as batting went. Hit .260, which is 10 to 20 points off his usual pace. In 1949 "Peewee" hit .279. Led the League in runs scored with 132. Hit 16 homers. Batted in 73 runs. Stole 26 bases. Led NL in fielding at short. In Navy 3 years. On 4 All-Star teams.   A DOVER REPRINT

No. 80 in the 1951 SERIES

BASEBALL
PICTURE CARDS

©1951 Bowman Gum, Inc., Phila., Pa., U.S.A.

TED KLUSZEWSKI

First Base—Cincinnati Reds
Born: Argo, Ill., Sept. 10, 1924
Height: 6-2   Weight: 225
Bats: Left   Throws: Left

One of the long ball hitters of the National League (slugging average, .515). Batted .307 for the 1950 Reds. Hit 37 doubles and 25 homers. Got 165 hits, good for 277 bases. Drove in 111 runs. In first year in baseball (1946) led the Sally League with a .352 average. In second year, led the Southern Association with a .377 average. With Cincinnati since 1948. Played football, U. of Indiana.

No. 143 in the 1951 SERIES

BASEBALL
PICTURE CARDS

©1951 Bowman Gum, Inc., Phila., Pa., U.S.A.
A DOVER REPRINT

PREACHER ROE

Pitcher—Brooklyn Dodgers
Born: Ash Flat, Ark., Feb. 26, 1918
Height: 6-1   Weight: 168
Bats: Right   Throws: Left

Recorded 19 wins and 11 losses in 1950 for a .633 percentage. Had a 15-6 record in 1949 and a percentage of .714, best in the League. Also had third most satisfactory earned run average (2.79). Chalked up the only Dodger victory in the 1949 World Series against the Yanks. With Cards and their farm teams, 1938-1943. With Pirates, 1944-1947. With the Dodgers since 1948.

No. 118 in the 1951 SERIES

BASEBALL
PICTURE CARDS

©1951 Bowman Gum, Inc., Phila., Pa., U.S.A.
A DOVER REPRINT

CURT SIMMONS

Pitcher—Philadelphia Phillies
Born: Egypt, Pa., May 19, 1929
Height: 5-11½   Weight: 178
Bats: Left   Throws: Left

By Sept. 2 of last season, Curt had piled up a 17-8 record. He was a cinch to be a 20-game winner. But his National Guard unit was activated. Off Curt went to the Army. He is considered one of the best pitching prospects discovered in recent years. The Phils landed him, after his graduation from high school. Pitched first big-league game on the last day of the 1947 season. A DOVER REPRINT

No. 111 in the 1951 SERIES

BASEBALL
PICTURE CARDS

©1951 Bowman Gum, Inc., Phila., Pa., U.S.A.

TED KLUSZEWSKI

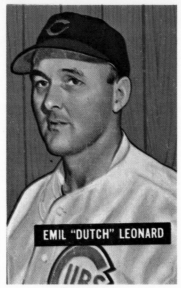

EMIL "DUTCH" LEONARD

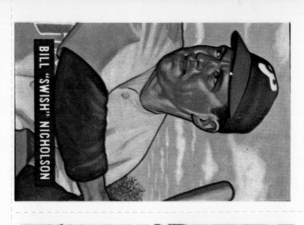

BILL "SWISH" NICHOLSON

PREACHER ROE

PHIL CAVARRETTA

LARRY JANSEN

WES WESTRUM

CURT SIMMONS

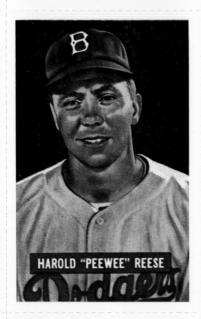

HAROLD "PEEWEE" REESE

SAL MAGLIE

CLYDE MC CULLOUGH

FRANK ROBINSON — Cincinnati Reds — 1B-O.F.

HEIGHT: 6:01 WEIGHT: 185 BATS: R THROWS: R
BORN: AUGUST 31, 1935 HOME: CINCINNATI, OHIO

MAJOR LEAGUE BATTING RECORD

	Games	At Bat	Runs	Hits	2B	3B	HR	RBI	Avg.
YEAR	146	540	106	168	31	4	36	125	.311
LIFE	596	2277	415	680	112	21	134	366	.299

SEASON'S HIGHLIGHTS

- APR. 9: Frank belts HR in opening day game.
- MAY 2: Drives in 5 runs vs. Dodgers.
- JUNE 23: Has perfect 4-for-4 day.

This is card number 490 of a set of 572 cards issued in 1960 by Topps Chewing Gum, Inc., of Brooklyn, New York, and is reprinted here by Dover Publications, Inc., of New York with the permission of the copyright holder, Topps.

FRANK BLASTED 3 HOMERS AGAINST THE PHILS IN A GAME LAST AUGUST

PRTD. IN U.S.A.

WILLIE DAVIS

HT: 6'2'' WT: 181 BATS: L
THROWS: L BORN: 4/15/40
HOME: LOS ANGELES, CALIF.

IN 1960, WILLIE WAS NAMED MINOR LEAGUE PLAYER OF THE YEAR.

This is card number 65 of a set of 664 cards issued in 1969 by Topps Chewing Gum, Inc., of Brooklyn, New York, and is reprinted here by Dover Publications, Inc., of New York with the permission of the copyright holder, Topps.

MAJOR AND MINOR LEAGUE BATTING RECORD

YEAR	TEAM	LEA.	G	AB	R	H	2B	3B	HR	RBI	AVG.
1959	Green Bay	I. I. I.	7	30	5	4	0	0	0	1	.133
1959	Reno	Calif.	117	513	135	187	40	16	15	90	.365
1960	Spokane	P. C. L.	147	624	126	216	43	26	12	75	.346
1960	Los Angeles	N. L.	22	88	12	28	6	1	2	10	.318
1961	Los Angeles	N. L.	128	339	56	86	19	6	12	45	.254
1962	Los Angeles	N. L.	157	600	103	171	18	10	21	85	.285
1963	Los Angeles	N. L.	156	515	60	126	19	9	6	60	.245
1964	Los Angeles	N. L.	157	613	91	180	23	7	12	77	.294
1965	Los Angeles	N. L.	142	558	52	133	24	3	10	57	.238
1966	Los Angeles	N. L.	153	624	74	177	31	6	11	61	.284
1967	Los Angeles	N. L.	143	569	65	146	27	9	6	41	.257
1968	Los Angeles	N. L.	160	643	86	161	24	10	7	31	.250
Major League Totals		9 Yrs.	1218	4549	599	1208	191	60	90	467	.266

©T.C.G. PRINTED IN U.S.A.

ROBIN E. ROBERTS — pitcher PHILADELPHIA PHILLIES

Ht: 6'1½" Wt: 190 Bats: R & L Throws: Right
Born: September 30, 1926; Springfield, Illinois

Although Robin's 1956 record fell off a little, he ranked 4th in Strikeouts and 2nd in fewest Walks. A blazing fastballer, he led the N.L. in Victories in 1952, 1954 and 1955.

This is card number 15 of a set of 411 cards issued in 1957 by Topps Chewing Gum, Inc., of Brooklyn, New York, and is reprinted here by Dover Publications, Inc., of New York with the permission of the copyright holder, Topps.

COMPLETE MAJOR LEAGUE PITCHING RECORD

YEAR	CLUB	LEA.	G	IP	W	L	PCT.	SO	BB	ERA
1948	Philadelphia	N. L.	20	147	7	9	.438	84	61	3.18
1949	Philadelphia	N. L.	43	227	15	15	.500	95	75	3.69
1950	Philadelphia	N. L.	40	304	20	11	.645	146	77	3.02
1951	Philadelphia	N. L.	44	315	21	15	.583	127	64	3.03
1952	Philadelphia	N. L.	39	330	28	7	.800	148	45	2.59
1953	Philadelphia	N. L.	44	347	23	16	.590	198	61	2.75
1954	Philadelphia	N. L.	45	337	23	15	.605	185	56	2.96
1955	Philadelphia	N. L.	41	305	23	14	.622	160	53	3.28
1956	Philadelphia	N. L.	43	297	19	18	.514	157	40	4.45
Major League Totals	9 Yrs.		359	2609	179	120	.599	1300	532	3.18

T. C. G. PRINTED IN U.S.A.

LOU BROCK — OUTFIELD ST. LOUIS CARDINALS

Ht: 5'11'' Wt: 170 Bats: Left Throws: Left
Born: June 18, 1939 Home: Bock Hill, Mo.

GOING ONE OF 5 MAJ. PLAYERS TO HIT A HOMER INTO THE POLO GROUNDS BLEACHERS

On June 15, '64, Lou SPARKED THE ST. LOUIS CARDINALS

Obtained from the Chicago Cubs on June 15, '64, Lou has sparked the St. Louis Cardinals' offense. He has used his great speed to upset opposing hurlers and start game winning rallies. Last season, Lou swiped 74 bases to lead the National League.

This is card number 285 of a set of 609 cards issued in 1967 by Topps Chewing Gum, Inc., of Brooklyn, New York, and is reprinted here by Dover Publications, Inc., of New York with the permission of the copyright holder, Topps.

MAJOR & MINOR LEAGUE BATTING RECORD

YEAR	TEAM	AB	R	H	2B	3B	HR	RBI	AVG.
1961	St. Cloud	501	117	181	33	6	14	82	.361
1962	Chicago	434	73	114	24	7	9	37	.263
1963	Chicago	547	79	141	19	11	9	37	.258
1964	Chi.-St. L.	634	111	200	30	14	14	58	.315
1965	St. Louis	631	107	182	35	8	16	69	.288
1966	St. Louis	643	94	183	24	12	15	46	.285
Maj. Totals 6 Yrs.		2900	821	822	132	56	63	245	.283

PRINTED IN U.S.A.

Richard Morrow GROAT — shortstop Pittsburgh Pirates

Dick will be a very welcome addition to the Pirates' roster in '55 when he rejoins the Bucs after 2 years in Service.

This is card number 26 of a set of 206 cards issued in 1955 by Topps Chewing Gum, Inc., of Brooklyn, New York, and is reprinted here by Dover Publications, Inc., of New York with the permission of the copyright holder, Topps.

Height: 6'
Weight: 175
Bats: Right
Throws: Right
Home: Swissvale, Penna.
Born: Nov. 4, 1930

MAJOR LEAGUE BATTING RECORD

	Games	At Bat	Runs	Hits	2b	3b	H.R.	R.B.I.	B. Avg.
Year				IN MILITARY SERVICE					
Life	95	384	38	109	6	1	1	29	.284

FIELDING

P.O.	Assists	Errors	F. Avg.
229	272	25	.952

?DAFFY-NITIONS

WHEN A PLAYER "HITS HIS WEIGHT," IS THAT GOOD?

ANS: Not unless he's very heavy. It usually means he's a poor hitter.

DON DRYSDALE — Pitcher L. A. Dodgers

HT: 6:06 WT: 205 THROWS: Right
BATS: Right BORN: July 23, 1936

This is card number 360 of a set of 576 cards issued in 1963 by Topps Chewing Gum, Inc., of Brooklyn, New York, and is reprinted here by Dover Publications, Inc., of New York with the permission of the copyright holder, Topps.

FINE HITTER, DON HIT 7 HOMERS IN 1958

COMPLETE MAJOR AND MINOR LEAGUE PITCHING RECORD

YEAR	TEAM	LEA.	G	IP	W	L	PCT.	SO	BB	ERA
1954	Bakersfield	Calif.	15	112	8	5	.615	73	53	3.45
1955	Montreal	Int.	28	173	11	11	.500	80	68	3.33
1956	Brooklyn	N. L.	25	99	5	5	.500	55	31	2.64
1957	Brooklyn	N. L.	34	221	17	9	.654	148	61	2.69
1958	Los Angeles	N. L.	44	212	12	13	.480	131	72	4.16
1959	Los Angeles	N. L.	44	271	17	13	.567	242	93	3.45
1960	Los Angeles	N. L.	41	269	15	14	.517	246	72	2.84
1961	Los Angeles	N. L.	40	244	13	10	.565	182	83	3.69
1962	Los Angeles	N. L.	43	314	25	9	.735	232	78	2.84
Major League Totals		7 Yrs.	271	1630	104	73	.588	1236	490	3.21

©T.C.G. PRINTED IN U.S.A.

MONFORD IRVIN

Home: Orange, N. J.
Born: Feb. 25, 1919, Columbia, Ala.
Ht.: 6'1'' — Wt.: 195
Bats: Right — Throws: Right

When Monty broke his ankle in the Spring of '52, Giant pennant hopes were dealt a severe blow. Monty came back at the end of the '52 season to lead the Giants in Batting. He was the top Hitter in the '51 World Series with 11 Hits and a .458 mark. Monty hit .300 in '50. In '51 he topped the NL with 121 RBI's and batted .312. The former Lincoln University star has been in organized baseball since 1949.

This is card number 62 of a set of 274 cards issued in 1953 by Topps Chewing Gum, Inc., of Brooklyn, New York, and is reprinted here by Dover Publications, Inc., of New York with the permission of the copyright holder, Topps.

DUGOUT QUIZ

When AL team holds the most total bases record for one game?

FIELDING RECORD

PUTOUTS	44 1254
ASSISTS	3 131
ERRORS	0 22
FIELD AVG.	1.000 .984

©T.C.G. PTD. IN U.S.A.

WILLIE MAYS — San Fran. Giants, outfield

HT: 5'11'' WT: 180 BATS: RIGHT THROWS: RIGHT
BORN: MAY 6, 1931 HOME: NEW YORK, N. Y.

COMPLETE MAJOR AND MINOR LEAGUE BATTING RECORD

YEAR	TEAM	LEA.	G	AB	R	H	2B	3B	HR	RBI	AVG.
1950	Trenton	Int.-St.	81	306	50	108	20	8	4	55	.353
1951	Minneapolis	A. A.	35	149	38	71	18	3	8	30	.477
1951	New York	N. L.	121	464	59	127	22	5	20	68	.274
1952	New York	N. L.	34	127	17	30	2	4	4	23	.236
1953	New York	N. L.				(Military Service)					
1954	New York	N. L.	151	565	119	195	33	13	41	110	.345
1955	New York	N. L.	152	580	123	185	18	13	51	127	.319
1956	New York	N. L.	152	578	101	171	27	8	36	84	.296
1957	New York	N. L.	152	585	112	195	26	20	35	97	.333
1958	San Francisco	N. L.	152	600	121	208	33	11	29	96	.347
1959	San Francisco	N. L.	151	575	125	180	43	5	34	104	.313
1960	San Francisco	N. L.	153	595	107	190	29	12	29	103	.319
Major League Totals		9 Yrs.	1218	4669	884	1481	233	91	279	812	.317

This is card number 150 of a set of 587 cards issued in 1961 by Topps Chewing Gum, Inc., of Brooklyn, New York, and is reprinted here by Dover Publications, Inc., of New York with the permission of the copyright holder, Topps.

DODGERS

WILLIE DAVIS
Outfield

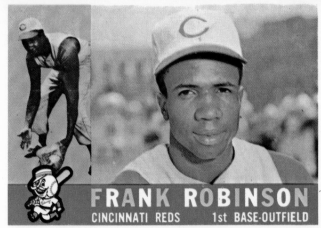

FRANK ROBINSON
CINCINNATI REDS   1st BASE-OUTFIELD

CARDS

LOU BROCK · OUTFIELD

ROBIN ROBERTS
PHILADELPHIA PHILLIES
P.

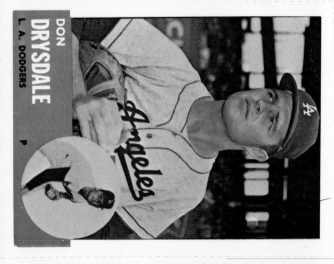

DON
DRYSDALE
L. A.
DODGERS

P

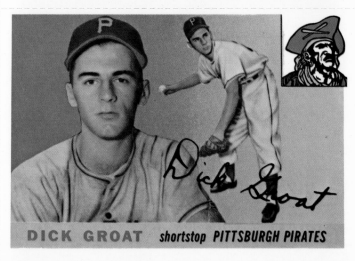

DICK GROAT   shortstop PITTSBURGH PIRATES

WILLIE MAYS
Outfield

San Francisco
Giants

MONTE IRVIN
outfielder NEW YORK GIANTS